SONIA FRIEDMAN PRODUCTIONS AND SCOTT M DELMAN
IN ASSOCIATION WITH TULCHIN BARTNER PRODUCTIONS,
LEE DEAN & CHARLES DIAMOND, 1001 NIGHTS,
JFL THEATRICALS / GHF PRODUCTIONS,
SCOTT & BRIAN ZEILINGER / JAMES LEFKOWITZ

PRESENT THE WEST END TRANSFER OF THE HEADLONG
AND ROYAL COURT THEATRE CO-PRODUCTION OF

THE NETHER

BY JENNIFER HALEY

The UK Premiere of THE NETHER took place at the Royal
Court Jerwood Theatre Downstairs, Sloane Square on
Thursday 17th July 2014.

Original Cast

Sims **Stanley Townsend**
Morris **Amanda Hale**
Doyle **David Beames**
Iris **Zoe Brough/Isabella Pappas**
Woodnut **Ivanno Jeremiah**

The development of THE NETHER was supported by the
Eugene O'Neill Theater Center during a residency at the
National Playwrights Conference 2011, Preston Whiteway,
Executive Director; Wendy Goldberg, Artistic Director.
THE NETHER was developed at the Lark Play Development
Center, NYC.

Center Theater Group / Kirk Do[uglas Theatre], Michael
Ritchie, Artistic Director, produ[ced]
THE NETHER in Los Angeles, CA

THE NETHER
BY JENNIFER HALEY

CAST (in order of appearance)

Sims **Stanley Townsend**
Morris **Amanda Hale**
Doyle **David Calder**
Iris **Jaime Adler/Zoe Brough/Perdita Hibbins/Isabella Pappas**
Woodnut **Ivanno Jeremiah**

UNDERSTUDIES

Sims/Doyle **Nigel Carrington**
Woodnut **Will Irvine**
Morris **Anna Martine**

Writer **Jennifer Haley**
Director **Jeremy Herrin**
Set Designer **Es Devlin**
Costume Designer **Christina Cunningham**
Video Designer **Luke Halls**
Lighting Designer **Paul Pyant**
Music by **Nick Powell**
Sound Designer **Ian Dickinson for Autograph**
Casting Director **Julia Horan CDG**

Associate Director **Des Kennedy**
Set Associates **Bronia Housman, Chiara Stephenson & Machiko Weston**
Video Associate **Jonathan Lyle**
Lighting Associate **David Howe**
Sound Associate **Luke Swaffield**
Casting Associate **Lotte Hines**
Resident Director **Daniel Raggett**

Production Manager **Tariq Rifaat**
Deputy Production Manager **Chris Mercer**
Company Stage Manager **Linsey Hall**
Deputy Stage Manager **Bonnie Morris**
Assistant Stage Manager **Cleo Maynard**
Costume Supervisor **Gayle Woodsend**
Wardrobe Mistress **Antonia Mellows**
Hair Sylist **Elaine Amielle**
Sound Operator **Jenn Goodheart-Smithe**
Chaperone **Elaine Henderson-Boyle**

The Royal Court, Headlong & Stage Management wish to thank the following for their help with this production:
Fran Bundey, Zoe Hurwitz.

THE NETHER
THE WRITER

Jennifer Haley

Theatre includes: **The Nether (Kirk Douglas Theatre, Los Angeles); Neighbourhood 3: Requisition of Doom (Humana Festival); They Call Her Froggy (Banff Centre/American Conservatory); Sustainable Living (Ojaj Playwrights Conference); Breadcrumbs (Contemporary American Theater Festival).**

Television includes: **Hemlock Grove.**

Awards include: **Ovation Award for Best Original Play (The Nether); LA Drama Critics Award for Writing (The Nether); Susan Smith Blackburn Prize (The Nether).**

Headlong

Headlong: /hedl'ong/ noun 1. with head first, 2. starting boldly, 3. to approach with speed and vigour

Headlong makes exhilarating theatre for audiences across the UK.

A touring company with a big imagination, we interrogate the contemporary world through a programme of fearless new writing, re-imagined classics and potent twentieth century plays. Via a combination of bold artistic leadership and the championing of visionary artists we are able to create spectacular work with the highest possible production values. By positioning the next generation of theatre makers alongside artists of international standing, Headlong ensures it consistently creates work that is bold and original.

In recognising the potential for technological innovation - through creative partnerships and the development of innovative digital content - Headlong continues to establish itself as a company for the digital age.

Artistic Director **Jeremy Herrin**
Executive Director **Henny Finch**
Finance Manager **Julie Renwick**
Administrative Producer **Fran du Pille**
Producer **Stephen Daly**
Administrator **Debbie Farquhar**
Creative Associate **Sam Potter**
Literary Associate **Duncan Macmillan**
Associate Artist **Sarah Grochala**
Marketing Consultant **Kym Bartlett**
Press Agent **Clíona Roberts**

www.headlong.co.uk
@HeadlongTheatre

Supported using public funding by
ARTS COUNCIL ENGLAND
LOTTERY FUNDED

Andrew Leung & Elizabeth Chan in Chimerica
Photo: Johan Persson

THE ROYAL COURT THEATRE

The Royal Court Theatre is the writers' theatre. It is the leading force in world theatre for energetically cultivating writers – undiscovered, new, and established.

Through the writers the Royal Court is at the forefront of creating restless, alert, provocative theatre about now, inspiring audiences and influencing future writers. Through the writers the Royal Court strives to constantly reinvent the theatre ecology, creating theatre for everyone.

We invite and enable conversation and debate, allowing writers and their ideas to reach and resonate beyond the stage, and the public to share in the thinking.

Over 120,000 people visit the Royal Court in Sloane Square, London, each year and many thousands more see our work elsewhere through transfers to the West End and New York, national and international tours, residencies across London and site-specific work.

The Royal Court's extensive development activity encompasses a diverse range of writers and artists and includes an ongoing programme of writers' attachments, readings, workshops and playwriting groups. Twenty years of pioneering work around the world means the Royal Court has relationships with writers on every continent.

The Royal Court opens its doors to radical thinking and provocative discussion, and to the unheard voices and free thinkers that, through their writing, change our way of seeing.

Within the past sixty years, John Osborne, Arnold Wesker and Howard Brenton have all started their careers at the Court. Many others, including Caryl Churchill, Mark Ravenhill and Sarah Kane, have followed. More recently, the theatre has found and fostered new writers such as Polly Stenham, Mike Bartlett, Bola Agbaje, Nick Payne and Rachel De-lahay and produced many iconic plays from Sarah Kane's **BLASTED** to Jez Butterworth's **JERUSALEM** and Laura Wade's **POSH**. Royal Court plays from every decade are now performed on stage and taught in classrooms across the globe.

It is because of this commitment to the writer that we believe there is no more important theatre in the world than the Royal Court.

Supported using public funding by
**ARTS COUNCIL
ENGLAND**

The Nether

Jennifer Haley is a playwright whose work delves into ethics in virtual reality and the impact of technology on our human relationships, identity and desire. *The Nether* won her the 2012 Susan Smith Blackburn Prize, a Los Angeles Ovation Award and Drama Critics Circle Award. Other plays include *Neighborhood 3: Requisition of Doom*, a horror story about suburban video-game addiction, and *They Call Her Froggy*, a noir thriller with interactive media design and a live soundtrack. Jennifer's work has been produced and developed at Center Theatre Group, the Royal Court Theatre, Actors Theatre of Louisville, American Conservatory Theater, The Banff Centre, Sundance Theatre Lab, the O'Neill National Playwrights Conference, Lark Play Development Center, PlayPenn, Page 73 Productions, and the MacDowell Colony. She is a member of New Dramatists in New York City and lives in Los Angeles, where she founded the Playwrights Union.

JENNIFER HALEY

The Nether

FABER & FABER

First published in 2014
by Faber and Faber Limited
74–77 Great Russell Street, London WC1B 3DA

The right of Jennifer Haley to be identified as author
of this work has been asserted in accordance with
Section 77 of the Copyright, Designs and Patents Act 1988

All rights whatsoever in this work, amateur or professional,
are strictly reserved. Applications for permission for any use
whatsoever, including performance rights, must be made in advance,
prior to any such proposed use, to Chris Till, Creative Artists Agency,
405 Lexington Avenue, 19th Floor, New York, NY 10174,
(phone: (212) 277-9000; email: chris.till@caa.com)

No performance may be given unless a licence has first been obtained

A CIP record for this book
is available from the British Library

Typeset by Country Setting, Kingsdown, Kent CT14 8ES
Printed and bound by CPI Group (UK) Ltd, Croydon, CR0 4YY

ISBN 978-0-571-31580-2

8 10 9 7

The Nether had its world premiere on 19 March 2013 at the Kirk Douglas Theatre, Los Angeles, California, produced by Center Theatre Group. The cast was as follows:

Sims Robert Joy
Doyle Dakin Matthews
Morris Jeanne Syquia
Woodnut Adam Haas Hunter
Iris Brighid Fleming

Director Neel Keller
Scene design Adrian W. Jones
Costume design Alex Jaeger
Lighting design Christopher Kuh
Sound design John Zalewski

The play received its European premiere in a co-production between Headlong and the Royal Court Theatre at the Royal Court Theatre, London, on 17 July 2014. The cast was as follows:

Sims Stanley Townsend
Doyle David Beames
Morris Amanda Hale
Woodnut Ivanno Jeremiah
Iris Zoe Brough, Isabella Pappas

Director Jeremy Herrin
Scene design Es Devlin
Costume design Christina Cunningham
Lighting design Paul Pyant
Sound design Ian Dickinson
Music Nick Powell
Video design Luke Halls

Characters

Sims/Papa
a successful businessman

Morris
a young female detective

Doyle
a middle-aged science teacher

Iris
a shining little girl

Woodnut
a fresh-faced guest

Time

Soon

Setting

An interrogation room and the Hideaway

THE NETHER

For Neel

NETHER REALM

1. Another world for mythical creatures

2. Demon world

3. A dimension of Evil or Imagination

urbandictionary.com

SCENE ONE

Interrogation Room.

Sims sits across a wide table from Detective Morris.

Sims I want to go home.

Morris Which home?

Sims I need to speak with my family.

Morris Which family?

Sims I don't know what you're getting at. I want my phone call.

Morris There are things we want, too.

Sims My lawyer.

Morris Which lawyer?

Sims Come on!

Morris You are free to contact whomever you wish, Mr Sims. We have a terminal here if you'd care to log in.

Sims

Morris I imagine your wife is worried by now.

Sims Leave her out of this.

Morris Your children.

Sims I don't have any children.

Morris You have a beautiful home, Mr Sims. Victorian. Set back from a country lane. Children on the front porch in long stockings and sailor caps. Barnaby. Donald.

Antonia. Iris. Such quaint names. From an era associated with . . . innocence.

Sims I have a brownstone. My wife is sterile. You've got the wrong guy.

Morris consults a report.

Morris Solicitation. Rape. Sodomy. Murder. These are heavy charges, Mr Sims.

Sims Are you charging me?

Morris The repetitive nature of the offences. The amount of money you've made.

Sims If you're not charging me –

Morris We know about your account in Burkina Faso.

Sims If you're not charging me, you have to let me –

Morris Oh, you're free to go.

Sims I'm free to go?

Morris We can't hold you here without charging you. That would be against the law.

Sims Okay. Then I'm going to go.

Morris We can't control a person's body. Yours is free to walk out the door.

Sims Great. My body is walking out the door.

Morris But if it does, we'll rescind your login, Mr Sims. You will never have access to a terminal again.

Sims Who did you say you are?

Morris This is an investigative unit of the Nether. I am an in-world representative. My name is Detective Morris.

Sims I have business in the Nether. All of my connections. You can't expel me.

Morris You have a taste for the old fashioned. Think of it as a return to simpler times.

Sims This is a violation of my rights. My lawyers are the best in the field. You won't keep me out for long.

Morris Long enough to locate and detain your children.

Sims

Morris What's wrong, Mr Sims?

Sims

Morris I thought you didn't have any children.

Sims

Morris We sent someone undercover to your realm to make sure our charges were grounded. Because you've programmed it so that nothing there may be recorded, he submitted a written report. (*Consulting a report.*) After undergoing a meticulous security scan of my login, creating my character from a set of prescribed 'looks', and passing a draconian manners tutorial dissuading modern terminology, I enter the Hideaway. The first thing I experience is the trees. The flickering light and soft sound as they sway in the sun and wind is almost overwhelming. They surround a beautifully rendered 1880s Gothic Revival with a squeak in the top porch step. I ring the doorbell. I can actually feel my hand sweat, clutching my carpetbag. I peek through a window and spy figures in the foyer – an impeccably dressed man stroking the face of one of the children, a little girl –

Sims They. Are not. Children.

Morris I guess that depends on context, Mr Sims. Or should I call you – Papa?

Interrogation Room.

Doyle sits across the table from Morris, head in his hands.

Morris Mr Doyle?

Doyle

Morris Mr Doyle.

Doyle

Morris Mr Doyle, we have not told your wife.

Doyle raises his head.

At this point we are merely detaining you. We need information about this man called Papa. In exchange, we will protect your identity.

(*Consulting a report.*) Cedric Doyle. You are a teacher at Franklin Middle School. You won a Distinguished Teaching Award in Science. You are one year away from retirement with full pension for forty years' service in the school district. Your wife is a senior vestry member of St Thomas Episcopal Church, where you used to teach Sunday school until about four years ago. You have one daughter, a junior at Illinois State.

(*Looking up.*) Footing the bill for an in-world college. That's a huge expense, Mr Doyle. Most students now get their higher education at online institutions in the Nether. You claim to moonlight as a professor at one of these institutions – the (*consulting the report*) University of Metaphysical Certitude.

If you like, this entire story about who you are may remain intact. We've even made arrangements with UMC to actually hire you. All those hours at your terminal, plus the boost in your bank account, will continue to make perfect sense.

Doyle May I keep her?

Morris Keep who?

Doyle Iris.

Morris No, Mr Doyle. Once we have what we need on Papa, that life is over.

Doyle

Morris

Doyle I have nothing to say.

SCENE THREE

Interrogation Room.

Morris and Sims.

Sims What authority do you have, yanking me from my garden?

Morris We thought face-to-face interaction would be a good change for you.

Sims You shouldn't even know who I am. I have the right to remain anonymous.

Morris We're able to track most of our users, but your identity encryption is like nothing we've ever seen. Once you log in, you disappear.

Sims Are you pissed you can't target me for advertising?

Morris We don't care about you, Mr Sims. It's your realm. The Hideaway. Have you heard of obscenity laws?

Sims My realm is properly registered and meets all international requirements.

Morris What about your server?

Sims My server?

Morris The physical machine where you store the code for the Hideaway.

Sims Yes, I know what it is.

Morris We want to know its location.

Sims My server is not in this country. So it's not any of your business.

Morris Your content is here. Your content is everywhere.

Sims It's not in your jurisdiction.

Morris Mr Sims, wherever your content appears is my jurisdiction.

Sims Since when?

Morris Your realm is not only popular, but lucrative. It's afforded you – *(consulting a report)* two hundred square feet of real grass, surrounding your brownstone. A garden of snap peas and swiss chard. Your wife's clothes are made from cotton. Why, with such in-world abundance, do you choose the life of a shade?

Sims I'm not a shade.

Morris Your login records indicate you spend a great deal of time online.

Sims You have a lot of work on your hands if that's become a crime.

Morris So you've never considered crossing over?

Sims I maintain my in-world life. I tend my garden.

Morris But really, Mr. Sims, an average of fourteen hours a day in the Nether? What can be gained by spending so much time in something that isn't real?

Sims Just because it's virtual doesn't mean it isn't real. Eighty per cent of the population work in office realms, children attend school in educational realms – there's a realm for anything you want to know or do or think you might want to try. As the Nether becomes our contextual framework for being, don't you think it's a bit out of date to say it isn't real?

Morris Is your wife aware of your tendencies?

Sims She asks no questions as long as the wine-made-from-grapes arrives at the door.

Morris Your tendencies toward children, Mr Sims.

Sims (*slight pause*) Like everyone, she's as aware as she wants to be.

Morris What if we made her very aware?

Sims I expect she would resent you.

Morris Or brought it to the attention of your neighbours?

Sims I don't spend enough time in-world to worry about my standing in the community. And my record is whistle clean. Real children are hard to come by these days. It's not like they play outside any more.

Morris Are you trying to be droll, Mr Sims?

Sims Yeah, I'm trying very hard to be very fucking droll.

Morris It won't reflect well on your case.

Sims Do I have a case here? A case sounds legal, which this definitely is not.

Morris We need you to give us the location of your server. When we have confiscated your hardware and deleted your realm, you'll be free to go without prosecution –

Sims This is against the law!

Morris Relax, Mr Sims.

Sims My realm is clearly designated Adult. There are adults behind the children and adults behind the guests. My background checks are thorough in the extreme to make sure we don't involve users who are underage. This is in accordance with the statute on concensual role play –

Morris You seem to be quite up on laws and statutes.

Sims It is my business –

Morris This is our business, too. The Nether is home to many businesses, with an obligation to protect the needs of our community. And our community has decided that realms such as yours are impermissible –

Sims (*sarcastic*) Was there a vote?

Morris A referendum. I suggest you pay greater attention to the message boards.

Sims This is shit. You're feeding me shit.

Morris Would you care to log in right now and check?

Sims So you can trace me to my server? No, I would not.

Morris Then you'll just have to trust I'm telling the truth.

Sims leaps to his feet.

Sims Trust you? Who are you?!

Morris The Nether is no longer some great Wild West. We have a political body that is just as real as anything in-world. And we're making our own laws, with our own form of prosecution. You ask what authority I have? Look around. There's no Hideaway here. Now I suggest you sit down.

Sims

Morris

He sits.

Sims Look, Detective, I am sick. I am sick and have always been sick and there is no cure. No amount of cognitive behavioural therapy or relapse determent or even chemical castration will sway me from my urges toward children. I am sick and no matter how much I loved him or her I would make my own child sick and I see this, I see this – not all of us see this – but I have been cursed with both compulsion and insight. I have taken responsibility for my sickness. I am protecting my neighbour's children and my brother's children and the children I won't allow myself to have, and the only way I can do this is because I've created a place where I can be my fucking self!

SCENE FOUR

The Nether. The Hideaway Foyer.

A ray of sunlight beams through a tall window. Papa enters as Iris runs in, breathless. He catches her, spins her around in the light. She shrieks with laughter. He puts her down, and she wobbles in circles.

Iris Whoa! I'm a top!

Papa Was that fun?

Iris Yes! I feel dizzy!

Papa I thought you'd like that. It's new.

Iris Have you given it a name?

Papa Not yet. Any ideas?

Iris I'd call it the Spinning Top.

Papa The Spinning Top it is.

Iris Did you try it on Barnaby?

Papa You're the first.

Iris I am?

Papa I knew you'd appreciate it the most. I need an easy audience to give me heart.

Iris (*suggestively*) Are you saying I'm easy?

Papa Now Iris . . . that joke is too old for you.

She giggles and reassumes innocence.

Iris I've never asked you for anything, have I, Papa?

Papa No, you haven't.

Iris I was thinking. I might want a birthday party.

Papa A birthday party?

Iris Yes.

Papa Are you trying to grow up? You're already nine years old.

Iris I imagined the yard dressed in streamers. And birthday cake. We could invite our favourite Hideaway guests.

Papa Involve the guests. So this is an entrepreneurial idea?

Iris Somewhat.

Papa Somewhat?

Iris Not altogether.

Papa Then what? You must tell me what's on your mind.

Iris I want a day that's all about me.

Papa

Iris

Papa Come here.

She moves to him.

We have a beautiful home here, Iris. We have a beautiful family, of which you are an important member. It is this beauty which draws our guests. And of course a sympathetic community. But do you know what is the most important thing we offer?

She shakes her head.

An opportunity to live outside of consequence.

She thinks this over.

Nothing here can change. Which is a beautiful reflection of the way we are changeless.

Iris Like the way God sees us.

Papa God?

Iris (*almost guiltily*) I've been thinking about God.

Papa I see.

Iris Not as in a person. But as in the way we are with each other. Do you think about God that way?

The sound of a grand doorbell is heard.

Papa We have a guest. You'd best go to the parlour.

Iris Yes, Papa.

She turns to go.

Papa Iris? I'm sorry we cannot have a birthday. It would upset a balance here to suggest you're growing older.

Iris I understand.

Papa I know you do. You're my darling girl.

Papa puts his hand to her cheek. Woodnut enters, and Papa quickly drops his hand. He gives Iris a gentle push, and she exits. Papa turns to Woodnut.

Papa My good sir! Welcome to the Hideaway!

Woodnut Thank you!

Papa Your first time?

Woodnut As a matter of fact, yes. Is it obvious?

Papa Not to worry. Keep coming back and you'll fit right in.

Woodnut You're confident I'll wish to return?

Papa I guarantee it, Mr . . .

Woodnut Woodnut. Thomas Woodnut. And you are . . .?

Papa You may call me Papa.

SCENE FIVE

Interrogation Room.

Morris and Doyle.

Morris (*reading from a report*) Papa escorts me to the parlour, where I find three of the children. A girl who looks to be twelve years old playing a perfectly rendered vintage Steinway pianoforte. A five-year-old boy dancing with a dandified guest. And the little girl I saw in the foyer – the one whose cheek Papa was stroking – sitting in a window seat. What is your name? I ask. She replies, My name is Iris. Without further discussion, she takes my hand and leads me up a grand staircase to the second floor.

We move down a darkened hallway, doors on both sides and the walls covered with weapons. From behind one door come the low sounds of what must be a fourth child, whimpering. Iris leads me to the last door off the hallway. Hanging above it, covered in dark red stains, is an axe.

We enter a bedroom with flowered wallpaper and a white lace bed. A little girl's dream. I case the joint in frank amazement, the detail of rendering – down to the smell of mulch rising from a garden beneath her window – throwing me into a state of pleasure and confusion. Iris beckons to me . . . Why don't you come here? I won't bite . . . She then circles her fingers around the bunny's ear, stroking from base to tip –

Doyle Okay.

Morris Okay what, Mr Doyle?

Doyle Do you think you're going to shame me into helping you? I'm past shame.

Morris Then why are you finding it hard to listen?

Doyle Because I'm sick of your voice. How old are you?

Morris Why do you ask?

Doyle You remind me of my students. So full of themselves. So sure they know what the hell is going on.

Morris I'll shut up if you give me the information I need on Papa.

Doyle I don't have information. We are anonymous to each other. I have no idea who he is other than how he presents himself in the Hideaway.

Morris Does your wife know about him?

Doyle

Morris Why don't we log in right now and contact her?

Doyle Fine.

Morris Fine?

Doyle My wife won't leave me.

Morris Your daughter?

Doyle I've saved enough money for her to finish college. And I don't care what she thinks of me. She's an adult now. She can think any thoughts she wants.

Morris Your job?

Puh. I was considered one of the top teachers in the country, an inspiration to future scientists. I turned down professorships to stay in the public system. I won awards. Then came the Single School Act, which consigned all lessons to educational games in the Nether. I became no more than an informant, monitoring the students' online escapades, making sure they weren't hacking through the school firewall to engage in porn . . .

Morris Is that how you discovered the Hideaway?

Doyle The advertising was compelling, to say the least. I wanted to see if they'd gotten it right with Victorian-era inventions.

Morris When you entered, were you aware of your proclivity?

Doyle What proclivity?

Morris Little girls.

Doyle The image of a little girl.

Morris It's more than that, Mr Doyle. It's sound, smell, touch. The Hideaway is the most advanced realm there is when it comes to the art of sensation.

Doyle Our bodies are ninety-nine per cent space. Physical sensation is inconsequential.

Morris As a scientist, how can you say that? Sensation is our gateway.

Doyle Yes? Gateway to what?

Morris To understanding the rules of the world.

Doyle The world we walk upon. But what about the world of our imagination?

Morris Exactly the same. People meet as physical beings in the Nether.

Doyle But there are no longer physical barriers to that contact. Now we may communicate with anyone, through any form we choose. And this communication – this experience of each other – is the root of consciousness. It is the universe wanting to know itself. Can't you see what a wonder it is that we may interact outside our bodies? It's as revolutionary as – discovering fire!

Morris And just as dangerous. Who are we when we 'interact' without consequence? What is revealed by feeling an axe slide through the flesh of a little girl?

Doyle The revelation is when she resurrects and comes to stand before you again. Images, sensations – those are fleeting. It's the relationships that matter.

Morris

Doyle

Morris You intend to cross over, don't you? I thought your affairs were in remarkable order. Of course you're not concerned with anything in-world. You were going to become a permanent shade.

Doyle

Morris That is an egregious step, Mr Doyle. And still highly experimental. You've probably looked into life-support systems. I can tell you from experience they're not half as good as they're advertised. I've seen bodies, after only one year, that are unrecognisable.

Doyle This bag of flesh is unrecognisable.

Morris We treat shades here. It is a long battle to get them to accept themselves again. The suicide rate is high. We have programmes –

Doyle I don't want your programmes.

Morris The desire to live as someone else is a symptom of depression.

Doyle I'm not depressed. I'm sad.

Morris What about your in-world relationships? What about your daughter?

Doyle I'll tell her where to find me.

Morris So she can come visit? A nice little family visit in the Hideaway?

Doyle We could stroll arm in arm down a country lane . . .

Morris Do you think Papa would allow that?

Doyle She would need to obey the rules of the realm, but absolutely.

Morris Our agent didn't find Papa so magnanimous. In fact he reports a rigid behavioural prescription –

Doyle Your agent listed facts in his report. But the next time you have a chat by the water-cooler, don't ask him, *What did you see? What did you do?* Ask him, *How free did you feel?*

SCENE SIX

Iris's Bedroom.

Iris stands with her stuffed rabbit as Woodnut inspects the room.

Woodnut This bedroom. It's beautiful. A little girl's dream.

Iris I'm glad you like it, Mr Woodnut.

He goes to the window.

Woodnut Sunshine. Warmth. Is that a garden down there?

Iris Snap peas. Swiss chard. Lemon basil.

Woodnut Is it seasonal?

Iris Absolutely. You are fortunate to visit us in late spring.

Woodnut Four seasons . . . adding up to a year?

Iris We don't think of it as 'adding up'. Nothing here truly changes.

Woodnut And whose idea was all of this?

Iris Papa's, of course.

Woodnut Papa? He is not merely a chaperone?

Iris Oh no, he created the Hideaway.

Woodnut He came up with the idea? And did the programming?

Iris We don't use that word here, Mr Woodnut.

Woodnut I apologise.

Iris It is your first time.

Woodnut

Iris Why don't you come here? I won't bite.

She circles the bunny's ear with her fingers, strokes it from base to tip. Woodnut clears his throat. He approaches her.

It's okay to be nervous.

Woodnut I'm not nervous.

Iris Go ahead then. Touch me.

Woodnut pats her stiffly on the head. She takes his hand and moves it over her face. He jerks his hand away.

Perhaps you'd like to start with the axe.

Woodnut I beg your pardon?

Iris That usually comes after, but if you're more inclined that way –

Woodnut No. No. I do not wish to start with the axe.

Iris Alright.

Woodnut Is it – expected?

Iris Papa prefers it for returning guests, but we don't have to do it the first time. Is there something else you'd like to play? I've got marbles, jacks, pick-up sticks . . .

Woodnut What are those?

Iris They are games. I can show you. How about jacks?

Iris produces a bag of jacks and kneels on the floor. She motions Woodnut over.

First I'm going to drop all the jacks. (*She does.*) Now, I'm going to bounce the ball, pick up a jack, and catch the ball again, with the same hand. (*She does.*) See? (*Again.*) Would you like to try?

Woodnut puts down the carpetbag and kneels. Iris hands him the ball. Woodnut clumsily bounces the ball, pecks at a jack. The ball goes bouncing off. Iris retrieves it, laughing.

You were close! Try again!

Intrigued, Woodnut gives the task his full attention. He snags a jack and catches the ball.

Woodnut Aha!

Iris Very good! My turn!

Iris scoops up two jacks, catches the ball.

Woodnut You took two of them!

Iris First you take one, then two, then three!

Woodnut Let me try.

Woodnut scoops up two jacks, catches the ball. Iris claps. Woodnut laughs, pleased with himself.

Iris You did it!

Woodnut I did it!

He suddenly stops, drops the ball, stands.

Iris Is something wrong?

Woodnut I have quite . . . forgotten myself.

He goes to the window, stands in the sunlight and shadows of leaves. He takes a deep breath.

Iris It's okay to do that here, Mr Woodnut. It's okay to forget who you think you are.

Iris lifts her dress over her head and stands in her knickers.

And discover who you might be.

Woodnut

Iris

Woodnut slowly moves toward her.

SCENE SEVEN

Interrogation Room.

Morris and Sims.

Morris (*reading from a report*) I approach the little girl and fold her into my arms. Her skin is covered in

29

goosebumps, which quickly fade in my embrace.
(*Looking up.*) The next section of the report is classified,
but our agent did collect the evidence we needed to
pursue this case. He confessed to me in person this
experience left him traumatised.

Sims Your agent. Who was he?

Morris That's not important. What's important is – we
know everything that goes on in your 'establishment'.
And I have been eager for this encounter, Mr Sims, so I
could ask: how can you, in good conscience, infect people
with this content?

Sims Infect? That's rather dire. People come to my realm
of their own free will.

Morris They're enticed by its beauty. By sensations they
can no longer experience in the real world.

Sims Is it my problem the real world no longer measures
up?

Morris I would say it's all of our problem. But who's
going to do anything about it when they're busy violating
children?

Sims What are you afraid of? Violence? Porn? Did you
know porn drives technology? The first photographs?
Porn. The first movies? Porn. The most popular content
when the Nether was called the internet? Porn. The urge,
Detective – the *urge* – as long as we are sentient, you
will never stamp that out. You must have spent time in
those collegiate fantasy realms . . . questing . . . killing
wicked demons and wild boars. And the sex . . . I've been
there . . . I've seen the cock bulges. In-world men are no
comparison, with their soft, interface hands. Don't tell
me you never fucked an elf.

Morris No, Mr Sims, I never fucked an elf.

Sims Come on, you're missing out. The point is – it doesn't matter whether you kill a boar or a demon. Whether you have sex with a child or an elf. It's nothing but images. And there is no consequence.

Morris Images – ideas – create reality. Everything around us – our houses, our bridges, our wars, our peace treaties – began as figments in someone's mind before becoming a physical or social fact.

Sims Are you accusing me of creating paedophiles? If anything, I'm giving them a place to blow off steam.

Morris You've created a culture of legitimization, telling them their desires are not only acceptable, but commendable. Do you know what your guests are doing in-world?

Sims Do you? I've read the studies. No one has been able to draw a conclusive correlation between virtual behaviour and actual offence –

Morris There won't be a distinction when everyone decides they'd rather cross over. We are at the edge of what could become a mass migration into the Nether.

Sims Is that my fault, too?

Morris Your code is the closest anyone has come to perfecting the art of sensation –

Sims My code?

Morris Spend enough time in the Hideaway, and you forget –

Sims You want my code.

Morris – you want to forget the world itself –

Sims You want to sell it to Disney.

Morris No, Mr Sims –

Sims Use it to create some insipid realm where you can brainwash users into buying shit.

Morris We give our users more credit than that.

Sims You track them like bloodhounds. Now you want to tell them what to do. Or rather, what not to do. What not to think. What not to feel.

Morris You said yourself – the Nether is becoming our contextual framework for being. If that happens, the same laws should apply –

Sims It's not the same *way* of being! It's imagination! People should be free in their own imagination! That is one place, at least, where they should have total privacy! I grant them that. My identity encryption is so profound, even I don't know who comes to the Hideaway. In fact, you couldn't have hacked it without my knowing . . . How on earth did you find me?

Morris There is a line, even in our imagination. You don't just offer images of children. You provide the sound and the smell and the touch of them.

Sims You found me through one of my users . . .

Morris Even the eyes look alive.

Sims One of my guests, one of my children . . .

Morris They believe themselves to be real.

Sims Iris. She started asking questions. After spending time with –

Morris They believe your love for them is real.

Sims Mr Woodnut! He's your agent. He got to Iris. What did he do to her?

Morris It's what you did to her, Mr Sims. And I assure you, there's been a consequence.

SCENE EIGHT

Iris's Bedroom.

Music spills from a gramophone. Woodnut is in his shirtsleeves. Iris stands on his feet. They waltz.

Iris One two three, one two three. Left foot three. Right foot three. Left foot three. Right foot three . . . you're getting it!

Woodnut Don't say that – you'll mess me up!

Iris You're doing better, Mr Woodnut. Much better than last time. And vastly improved since we started.

Woodnut It's the dancing shoes. I bought them with my returning guest credit.

Iris It's also you. You're starting to feel it. Can't you tell?

Woodnut Yes . . . yes . . .

Iris I do believe you're a natural . . .

The music ends. Woodnut spins her around. She shrieks with delight. He puts her down and she wobbles.

Whoa! I feel . . . I feel . . .

Woodnut Dizzy?

Iris Happy!

Woodnut Me too!

They beam at each other. Then a slight apprehension comes over Woodnut. He takes the record off the gramophone, holds it up.

Where does the music come from?

Iris From the grooves. Can you feel them?

Woodnut Why yes. Yes, I can. But how are they turned into sound?

Iris You place the needle at the edge, and it follows what is actually a single groove that spirals all the way to the centre of the record, picking up vibrations.

Woodnut How do the vibrations get there?

Iris The reverse process. A sound is made, and they are etched into a master record.

Woodnut And then how do we hear them again?

Iris They go through the needle and hit a diaphragm at the base of the horn, which amplifies the sound.

Woodnut My goodness! It's all hardware!

Iris clears her throat pointedly.

I beg your pardon – I mean – it's all mechanical!

Iris Yes, it is!

Woodnut It's incredible what we have done using the materials of the earth. Not only have we built roads and cities, but we have created tools for our imagination.

Iris It's like magic.

Woodnut Exactly. Although I think we must be careful about letting the magic sweep us away, to the point where we forget where it came from. I personally like to have these . . . materials . . . to hold on to. Something tangible. I don't know what happens when the music plays, but I like being able to touch the grooves. Even when it comes to people.

Iris People?

Woodnut Yes. I may feel a certain way about someone and think they feel the same way about me, but how do I know it's mutual?

Iris Don't you trust the feeling?

Woodnut Not entirely. Take Papa, for example.

Iris What about Papa?

Woodnut You care for him a great deal.

Iris I do.

Woodnut Does he feel the same way about you?

Iris Of course.

Woodnut How do you know?

Iris Because of what he shares with me.

Woodnut What he shares with you here. But it's easy here. I only bring this up because, you see, my father was a shade –

Iris Mr Woodnut! Not only is that the second time you have used a forbidden word, but this subject of conversation –

Woodnut – is entirely against the rules – I know. But sometimes you go out of bounds with someone you care about. Let me just say, even if my father had shown me affection in the world of his imagination, even if we had danced together in the beautiful music of our minds, what I needed most from him, what I felt would truly express his love, was him entrusting me with something – even a small thing – that was real.

Iris mulls this over, troubled. Papa enters.

Papa Iris, have you forgotten our afternoon together?

Iris Oh! Is it afternoon already?

Papa Yes, it is. Mr Woodnut, you've quite gone over your time.

Woodnut Have I now? Iris, you should have told me.

35

Iris I forgot.

Papa You forgot?

Iris We were having fun.

Papa (*flustered*) Well, don't let me interrupt –

Iris Wait, Papa!

She goes to Papa, puts her hand in his.

Thank you, Mr Woodnut. That will conclude our time.

SCENE NINE

Interrogation Room.

Morris and Doyle. Doyle is weary, resigned to the questioning.

Morris I gather from our agent's report it was forbidden for members of the Hideaway to give out information about their real lives.

Doyle Correct.

Morris Did anyone, as far as you know, break the rules?

Doyle No.

Morris Papa? Did he ever break the rules?

Doyle No.

Morris Are you sure?

Doyle I'm tired.

Morris Mr Doyle, I must ask you to sit up.

Doyle straightens, resentfully.

So. You first came to the Hideaway as a guest?

Doyle Correct.

Morris How did you choose to appear?

Doyle Younger. I had thick hair the colour of wheat.

Morris At what point did you become close to Papa?

Doyle Almost immediately. Sometimes I'd go to the Hideaway just to visit with him.

Morris What would the two of you do?

Doyle Play billiards. Drink cognac. Talk.

Morris What did you talk about?

Doyle Industrialisation. The amazing steam engine.

Morris So this was all in character?

Doyle If that's how you need to frame it.

Morris But inventions were a popular topic?

Doyle Yes.

Morris And what did the two of you deduce?

Doyle About what?

Morris Human invention? Progress?

Doyle That we are trying to cast off the limitations of physicality and become pure spirit.

Morris Is that how you see crossing over? Becoming pure spirit?

Doyle Something like that.

Morris But Papa's realm demands form. A set of prescribed 'looks'.

Doyle The guests may choose from a wide range of appearance selections.

Morris What about the children? Do they have a choice?

Doyle The children are employees.

Morris What about Iris? Was she there when you arrived?

Doyle No. Another little girl.

Morris Another little girl?

Doyle Henrietta.

Morris Did she look like Iris?

Doyle Yes.

Morris Even though someone else was behind her?

Doyle Of course.

Morris So all of the children, no matter who is behind them, look the same.

Doyle The guests enjoy continuity.

Morris That sounds like something Papa would say. Who was it before Henrietta?

Doyle I don't know.

Morris And before her. And before her. Who was the first little girl?

Doyle I never asked.

Morris I wonder if she was someone real.

Doyle That's pure speculation.

Morris Speculation is my job. What happened to Henrietta?

Doyle She went to boarding school.

Morris Boarding school?

Doyle That's what . . . Papa said.

Morris Isn't that what happens when children do something naughty? Get sent away?

Doyle Maybe her behinder needed to move on.

Morris Maybe she broke the rules. Maybe she got too close to Papa.

Doyle All of the children are close to Papa.

Morris But does he have a favourite?

Doyle Well, there are always those beings to whom you are particularly drawn.

Morris

Doyle

Morris Did you tell Papa about your intention to cross over?

Doyle No.

Morris Why not? From the looks of your financial documents, you've been prepared for months.

Doyle It's a big decision. I've needed to deliberate –

Morris Has anyone crossed into the Hideaway? Children or guests?

Doyle I don't know.

Morris Has Papa?

Doyle I don't know.

Morris Was he ever gone when you logged in?

Doyle He could have been somewhere else in the Nether, doing business –

Morris But wasn't the topic open for discussion? If you're part of Papa's big, happy family, wouldn't he want to have at least some of you there permanently?

Doyle You weren't there. You don't know how it works –

Morris You've been there for years – why haven't you once brought it up? Unless you're not so sure of his response. Unless you're secretly afraid that if you offer yourself up to him, he'll punt you off to boarding school –

Doyle Look, you can do the hard-boiled baloney on me all you want, but I know – I know – what's in his heart!

SCENE TEN

A Sunny Spot.

Papa and Iris sit beneath a vault of trees. The sound of leaves fluttering is heard. Beside Papa is a huge box.

Iris . . . And Barnaby said Antonia shoved him. And Donald wasn't saying anything because his shorts were dirty too. The thing is it was Antonia's idea all along. She wanted to find out if the eggs *feel* warm when they've just come out of the chicken, and I said why didn't you ask me – I could have told you they do. And she said just because I'm Papa's favourite doesn't mean I should put on airs, and I said I'm not your favourite. Look how after the spanking room you kept stroking Donald's face and gave him that candy that's only for guests!

Papa Why do you get jealous?

Iris Not me. Antonia.

Papa I mean all of you. Don't you believe there's enough affection to go around?

Iris Maybe . . .

Papa Love is not like a sack of corn. You don't run out of it the more you give away.

Iris I know.

Papa And you can't believe everything she says. You are too trusting, my dear.

Iris Isn't that something you like about me?

Papa I just want you to be careful.

Iris I know.

Papa (*humoured*) I know, I know . . . you know everything, don't you?

Iris I know I must be a little bit special, to get to spend an afternoon with you.

Papa Well, of course you are special. It seems one of our guests has noticed it, too.

Iris You mean Mr Woodnut?

Papa You've been spending quite a bit of time with him.

Iris He's fascinated by what you've done here. He asks all kinds of questions.

Papa What does he ask?

Iris About you and how everything works.

Papa About me?

Iris I can't say I don't encourage him.

Papa Has Mr Woodnut availed himself of the axe?

Iris I don't think he's inclined in that direction.

Papa He's a returning guest. Perhaps you should give him a nudge.

Iris Shouldn't we let guests come to things on their own time?

Papa It keeps them from getting too close. That's something you should watch, as well. It makes you vulnerable and could upset a balance.

Iris Are you jealous?

Papa Iris!

Iris I'm just teasing, Papa. You know you're my favourite.

Papa

Iris Did you bring me something?

Papa Maybe.

Iris Is it a birthday cake?

Papa Let's call it an Iris Day cake.

Iris I want to see!

*He lifts the cover. The cake is beautiful, multi-tiered.
It looks like glass.*

Oooo!

Papa It's made of ice that will never melt.

Iris I can hear it. It's the sound of freezing and unfreezing.

Papa The cake reforms its crystal patterns.

Iris And there's another sound. The sound of tiny
dwarves who live in snowy mountains singing falsetto.

Papa leans in to the cake.

Can you hear it?

Papa No. I can't. It must be only for children to hear.

Iris Is that why you don't want me to grow up?

Papa Why?

Iris Because I'll no longer hear the singing?

Papa Because I don't want to lose you.

Iris It wouldn't be good for business.

Papa That's not why. You know why. Don't you?

Iris I feel it, but . . . I do sometimes wonder if it's real.

Papa

Iris

Papa Come here, Iris Day Girl.

She scoots closer.

Did you know these trees are called poplars?

Iris Yes.

Papa No you didn't!

Iris Yes I did!

He tickles her. Overlapping 'No you didn't!' / 'Yes I did!' as they giggle.

I promise! I did!

Papa Okay, I believe you! So here's a secret: I have a garden.

Iris Our garden?

Papa No, my own garden.

Iris What's in it?

Papa The same things that are growing in ours. And guess what I just planted? I've scoured the world for it.

Iris What?

Papa A sapling. A poplar.

Iris That's real?

Papa Real real.

Iris (*moved*) Thank you.

Papa Don't tell the others.

*She shakes her head emphatically. They sit for a
moment, listening to the wind in the leaves.*

There were poplars growing by our vacation cottage. It
was the last grove in the country. I would wake to my
bedroom wall aglitter with sunshine, the sound of wind
washing through the leaves, and my mother at the
window. She said, The only way you hear the wind is if it
has leaves to blow through.

Iris I miss the trees.

Papa I do too.

Iris I love you.

Papa hesitates.

SCENE ELEVEN

Interrogation Room.

Morris and Sims.

Morris You cultivate a parade of little girls, each looking
like the one before. You let them get close, but not too
close. When they start expressing real emotion, it's off to
boarding school.
  The guests choose from a set of looks that you provide.
The children look the same, no matter who's behind
them. The way everything appears is completely under
your control.
  You create a realm irresistible to anyone with a longing
for beauty, go there each day, play the music, pull the
strings, and force everyone else to dance to your
nightmare.

Sims I don't force anyone to do anything. Your agent –
Woodnut – knows that.

44

Morris It's here in the report. What you made him do.

Sims He got close to a little girl. He had sex with her. That's a highly illegal act for a member of law enforcement, but perhaps the Nether community has deemed it permissible?

Morris In the interest of collecting evidence –

Sims He could have collected evidence in one visit. He kept coming back.

Morris He needed more information.

Sims He came back because he liked it.

Morris He followed protocol and conducted a successful operation. Your presence here is proof of that.

Sims I think he even fell in love. He brought Iris flowers –

Morris Why do the girls look the same?

Sims And then she started asking about the other little girls . . .

Morris Iris. Henrietta. They're always the same and always your favourite.

Sims She was gone for three days . . . She came back and she was – crying –

Morris Who was the first little girl? Was she someone real?

Sims suddenly moves toward her.

Sims Tell me what happened to Iris.

Morris Give me the location of your server.

Sims What did you do to her?

Morris Give me the location, and I'll tell you what your psychosis has wrought.

Sims *My* psychosis? What is all of this to *you*? You clearly abhor shades. Maybe Mummy and Daddy spent too much time online and didn't pay enough attention to you? Personal insecurity draws you to law enforcement. Rookie detective, finds a home with 'an investigative unit of the Nether' – whatever the hell that is. Some shadow group that's got a few thugs, an interrogation facility and the entire population by their short and curly logins. And so pure you never even fucked an elf. Have you ever fucked anything, Detective? In-world or otherwise? *(Reaches for her.)* Have you ever been –

Morris Don't touch me.

He stops.

You don't know what I've done. And don't position yourself as someone who's protecting Iris. I don't know who the first little girl was, or what you did to her, but using her image revictimises her over and over again. Your concern is an act. Like Papa's kindness is an act. There is no love in your realm. There is only your ego. You even look like yourself in the Hideaway. And if people don't do what you want, you –

Sims How do you know what I look like in the Hideaway?

Morris

Sims

Morris Our agent made a positive ID.

Sims You made a positive ID.

Morris No, Mr Sims –

Sims Oh, yes. We had a chat over cognac. I recognise you.

SCENE TWELVE

The Hideaway Foyer.

Late-afternoon sun pours through the window. Woodnut enters, whistling. He wears a fancy new jacket and carries a bouquet of flowers. He preens in a wall mirror. Papa enters, carrying an axe. Woodnut's joviality evaporates.

Woodnut Papa.

Papa Good afternoon, Mr Woodnut.

Woodnut I have a visit with Iris.

Papa She's been delayed by another guest.

Woodnut I see.

Papa It seems you're not the only one who favours her.

Woodnut

Papa Cognac?

Woodnut Um. Certainly.

Papa casually puts down the axe, goes to a side table, pours two glasses of cognac, hands one to Woodnut.

Papa Cheers.

They drink.

Woodnut Oh my. This is strong.

Papa Aged fifty years.

Woodnut How do you do it?

Papa Perfecting this world is my obsession.

Woodnut Do you think obsession is required?

Papa For perfection?

Woodnut For making the world as you think it should be.

47

Papa Oh yes.

Woodnut I tend to agree. To what do I owe the honour of a drink?

Papa You've taken a shine to Iris. I've taken a shine to you.

Woodnut She's winsome.

Papa She's the best I've found.

Woodnut The best . . . of what?

Papa Suffice to say that all of one's children are cherished, but sometimes there is a favourite.

Woodnut I'm treating her quite well, if that's what you're concerned about.

Papa It is my concern. You should be careful about getting attached.

Woodnut This is merely a diversion.

Papa You visit quite a bit for a mere diversion. And I've noticed you've not yet – (*indicating the axe*) proceeded with the relationship.

Woodnut Is that entirely necessary?

Papa For returning guests, it shows a desire to partake fully of what we offer here.

Woodnut And what is that?

Papa A life outside of consequence.

Woodnut

Papa Is that not something you can subscribe to, Mr Woodnut?

Woodnut It is something I find hard to believe is possible. You see, my father was a shade . . . I beg your pardon. The cognac is having an effect.

48

Papa It hits hard if you're unaccustomed to it. But go on.

Woodnut I'm afraid I may break the rules.

Papa This one time, I give you leave.

Woodnut He never looked at me when I was a child. He never touched me. He never took me outside. All I remember is his body on life support, curling up. When he died, I found he'd listed me as the beneficiary of his login. I entered the Nether as him and found a single realm – a small, cosy room with an armchair and a fire. Over the mantel was a round mirror with my reflection, a wizened gargoyle. On a table next to the armchair was a book of poems by Theodore Roethke, with one passage highlighted:

> Dark, dark my light, and darker my desire.
> My soul, like some heat-maddened summer fly,
> Keeps buzzing at the sill. Which I is *I*?
> A fallen man, I climb out of my fear.
> The mind enters itself, and God the mind,
> And one is One, free in the tearing wind.

Papa

Woodnut

Papa I see why Iris likes you.

He downs the rest of his cognac.

Mr Woodnut, you have been asking questions about me. I must request you desist. And unless you want me to consider your activities here suspect, I suggest you . . . move along with the programme.

He puts one hand on Woodnut's arm, fatherly, and holds the axe out to him with the other.

Maybe this will help you climb out of your fear.

SCENE THIRTEEN

Iris's Bedroom.

Evening now. Woodnut stands before Iris with axe and flowers.

Iris It's okay, Mr Woodnut. I always resurrect.

Woodnut I don't want to do this.

Iris What are you afraid of?

Woodnut Will it hurt you?

Iris I feel only as much pain as I want.

Woodnut How much pain is that?

Iris That's rather a personal question.

Woodnut It's so beautiful here. Why do we have to bring in something terrible?

Iris Beautiful. Terrible. It's like life.

Woodnut Except that it isn't.

Iris It's an opportunity to do something you could never do otherwise.

Woodnut I have already been with you in ways that –

Iris That's one side. This is the other. Creation. Destruction. You begin to realise they're on the same wheel.

Woodnut I've interacted with some of the other guests. This technique does not seem to have set them on a path to enlightenment.

Iris People come to things on their own time. We offer a place where you may dismantle everything the world has told you about right and wrong and discover pure relationship.

Woodnut I don't think this is Papa's plan. I think it's yours.

Iris That's not true. He created this place –

Woodnut Papa did not create this place to foster pure relationship. I think you've made that up to justify wanting to stay here.

Iris Mr Woodnut!

Woodnut He does not love you.

Iris He does!

Woodnut You think because you feel love, so does everyone else –

Iris It's not just a feeling! He gave me something.

Woodnut jerks.

Woodnut What did he give you?

Iris Just like you said. He told me something real.

Woodnut Something from his real life?

Iris Yes! I asked him, and he told me.

Woodnut What was it? What did he say?

Iris I cannot tell you.

Woodnut You must. You must tell me what he said.

Iris I cannot tell a soul.

Woodnut Don't you trust me?

Iris Of course I do. And Papa trusts me!

Woodnut He doesn't trust you, he controls you. He controls everything! He sits at his terminal and makes you dance at the end of his strings!

Iris That's not true! And I must remind you of the –

51

Woodnut – rules! Yes, all of the rules here! Rules about saying too much! Rules about getting too close! It's supposed to be about freeing yourself, and yet nothing is truly free –

Iris Mr Woodnut, I would kill myself if I betrayed him!

Woodnut Okay. Okay. I cannot make you see.

He flings himself on to the window seat and sulks. Iris mulls. Finally:

Iris I cannot give you Papa's offering. But I can give you one of mine.

Woodnut Isn't that against the rules?

Iris Yes.

Woodnut Alright.

Iris I won a Distinguished Teaching Award in Science.

Woodnut

Iris

Woodnut (*earnest*) Congratulations.

Iris Thank you.

Woodnut Thank you.

She gives him a long hug. He touches his eyes. Startled to find them wet. He jumps up.

I think I understand why Papa wants this. It's so we don't get too attached. And maybe he's right. Maybe I should not get too attached.

He retrieves the axe, turns to Iris.

Come here.

Interrogation Room.

Doyle and Morris.

Morris (*reading from a report*) And in those moments, standing in the carnage of her small body, the hot smell of everything we have inside rising around me, I stare at the blood on my hands and think, my God, look at the brightness of it, look at the bright beauty, how does this exist in nature, how does it exist in any way, in any code I can understand? I look down to find her body gone. What have I done, have I done something, have I done nothing, is this all nothing, is everything nothing? A giggle at the door, and she reappears, coming toward me with her arms open – and I lift the axe and do it again. And I do it again. And I do it again. I want her to stop coming so I know I've done something. But she keeps coming, and now it's not just my hands covered in blood, it's my face, it's my body, I can taste it in my mouth, it's so exquisite I am crying, I have never felt so much with every nerve, felt so much, felt so much . . . feeling. Until I'm spent. And she comes to me again, eyes wide. But if there has been no consequence, there has been no meaning – no meaning between her and myself, between myself and myself – and if there has been meaning, then I am a monster. (*Looking up.*) Our agent was too distraught to return after this visit, and so, Mr Doyle, we decided to bring you in.

Doyle Your agent . . . your agent was Mr Woodnut . . .

Morris Yes.

Doyle The Science Award . . .

Morris We investigated previous winners until we found someone with an excessive login time and an offshore bank account.

Doyle . . . I trusted him . . .

Morris He came to care for you. Very much.

Doyle He didn't care for me. He ruined me.

Morris He wanted to help you.

Doyle And I did nothing wrong. I've done nothing wrong.

Morris The Hideaway is wrong. You're a part of that.

Doyle It draws people who are – broken. I know that, but – I don't judge them. They are part of us, too – they are part of the world. God does not judge them – why should we?

Morris You fell into a relationship – it's emotional – I understand –

Doyle Do you? Do you understand?

Morris This man you call Papa does not feel for you as you do for him.

Doyle I know he does.

Morris He's obsessed with an image he created.

Doyle It's more than that.

Morris Whose idea was it that you transition from guest to little girl?

Doyle Papa's.

Morris He could only become intimate with you in that form.

Doyle No! I had . . . spent all of our money. It was a way for me to stay in the Hideaway. He came up with a perfect solution.

Morris He'd been grooming you because Henrietta was getting too close. Everything he does is for his ego.

Murdering children does not keep you from getting too close, it makes you complicit.

Doyle You don't know this! You don't know anything! He gave me something real.

Morris What was it?

Doyle I'm not telling you! You may have me, but you won't get Papa.

Morris He had something real to give you! Something from his real life! He doesn't live in the Hideaway – he's not crossing over – why would you?

Doyle I don't want to be here any more.

Morris What about your daughter? Have you really told your daughter?

Doyle She is an adult now – I am not responsible –

Morris You are! You are responsible to her for ever!

Doyle I'll tell her where to find me –

Morris In the Hideaway, Mr Doyle? My father was a shade, and what I wanted most from him was a relationship here on this earth!

Doyle looks at her hard. His mouth drops.

Doyle . . . I trusted *you* . . .

Morris

Doyle

Morris

Doyle

Morris Listen, I will to allow you to see Papa again. If he loves you – you – and wants you to cross, I'll let you stay in the Hideaway together. If not, you will give me what you have on him.

Doyle How could I trust you again?

Morris Mr Doyle, you have been the greatest surprise of my professional life. You are my . . . first love, if you can imagine that. What Papa's doing is wrong. It's hurting you. And I . . . can't bear to see that. This is the offer I'm allowed to make. I'll stake my career on it. Take it, or you'll never see him again. And then how will you know what's in his heart?

Doyle

Morris Come, Mr Doyle, let's log in.

Morris and Doyle become . . .

SCENE FIFTEEN

. . . Woodnut and Iris.

Iris' Bedroom.

Iris is shivering.

Woodnut Are you cold? Would you like me to –

Iris No. Don't touch me, Detective.

Woodnut He's coming. I'll be here, behind the door.

Woodnut hides. Papa enters.

Papa There you are, my child! Where have you been?

Iris I have had a fever.

Papa For three days?

Iris I'm afraid so.

Papa Why didn't you send me word?

Iris Papa, I have to ask you a question.

Papa Of course.

Iris The girls before me. Like Henrietta.

Papa What of them?

Iris Did you feel about them the way you do me?

Papa I don't understand.

Iris Why do we all look alike?

Papa You know the guests enjoy continuity.

Iris The guests, Papa? Or you?

Papa Are you being impertinent?

Iris Who was the first?

Papa The first what?

Iris The first little girl? Was she someone you knew?

Papa Iris. In a moment of affection, I gave you a small piece of something real, but asking this of me – you go too far.

Iris I'm sorry, Papa.

Papa You know we have rules here.

Iris I respect the rules. I would live with them entirely. I want to cross over.

Papa You want to cross?

Iris Wouldn't you like to have me here permanently?

Papa I need to remind you this is a business.

Iris Is that all it is?

Papa No, but objectivity is required to keep us afloat.

Iris But am I special to you?

Papa Of course. Haven't I made that clear?

Iris Am I special, not just as Iris?

Papa You are Iris.

Iris No, I am more than that. I am more than something you've made. Do you love me?

Papa

Iris

Papa I don't think you should cross. Take a few days off, come back, and we'll forget this conversation ever happened. If you find yourself unable to forget, it may be time for boarding school.

Iris starts weeping.

Iris. Iris, stop that. Stop it right now. I did not build the crying function for this purpose. Iris! This is exactly what I am talking about! This is the problem with getting too close! Iris, do as I say!

He slaps her. Long pause.

Iris Mr Woodnut once asked me if I feel pain. And I said to him, only as much as I want. But I see now, that's not quite the pain he meant.

Papa (*anguished*) Is there anything I can do to make it up to you?

Iris (*slowly*) You could tell me one more time about your secret.

Papa I have a garden, with a poplar. One of the last in the world.

Iris Thank you.

Papa Certainly.

Iris I'm sorry.

Papa You don't need to apologise.

Iris Yes, Papa, I do.

She sniffles, pulls herself together.

Now if you don't mind, I have guests.

Papa Of course.

Papa reaches out to touch her affectionately, but she only puts out her hand, businesslike. They shake.

It is good to have you back and working.

An awkward pause. Papa exits. Woodnut emerges.

Woodnut (*gently*) You did very well.

Iris stands in an attitude of dejection.

I know that was hard. I'm sorry. I really am.

Iris stands. Woodnut moves to the window.

Once, sitting here, I thought I had a memory of my father, holding me up to a window . . . I looked out and, on the horizon, saw the sun coming through a thin line of trees. I'd always assumed I was too young to remember trees. And I'm not sure if, sitting here, I didn't make that memory up. But either way, I must admit, it gives me comfort.

He turns to Iris.

I will make sure you and your family are looked after. Everything I said, back in the room, was real.

Iris's only movement is a sort of mechanical breath.

Are you alright?

No response. He goes to her.

Iris?

He touches her. No response.

Mr Doyle. Mr Doyle.

Morris returns halfway to herself and finds Doyle missing from the interrogation room.

Woodnut/Morris Mr. Doyle!

SCENE SIXTEEN

Interrogation Room.

Morris and Sims.

Sims What did you do to her?

Morris It's what you did.

Sims The last time I saw her, she was crying.

Morris Why was she crying?

Sims She was crying because . . . the poplar . . .

Morris Saplings are exceedingly rare. It was easy to track the shipments.

Sims You used her to get that out of me.

Morris Mr Sims, Iris was a sixty-five-year-old man.

Sims Stop. We have the right to remain anonymous.

Morris He was a middle-school science teacher with a wife and a daughter.

Sims It is unethical for you to reveal –

Morris His name was Cedric Doyle.

Sims   – to reveal her identity to me!

Morris What are you afraid of? Are you unable to accept him in his true form?

Sims That's not her true form –

Morris It is, Mr Sims. It was.

Sims What do you mean – it was?

Morris We brought him here for questioning. After three days we sent him back to the Hideaway to get the information we needed. And then . . . before we knew what he was doing . . . he disengaged from our terminal and hanged himself.

Sims What?

Morris With his belt. The day before we brought you here.

Sims

Morris

Sims

Morris

Sims You killed her.

Morris No, you did.

Sims You had sex with her. You liked it.

Morris You led him on.

Sims I made a place where she was happy.

Morris His happiness wasn't about the place. It was about you. He thought you loved him.

Sims And you told her I didn't.

Morris I let you do that.

Sims You don't know what's in my heart!

Morris Do you?

Sims I meant everything I said to Iris. I – cared –

Morris Would you have cared about him as an old man?

Sims That wasn't who she was –

Morris Yes, that's who he was. He was in the body God gave him.

Sims God? You stand in this room and speak of God?

Morris As in what we are given. What we are made of. The materials of the earth.

Sims Aren't we more than that? Iris said she believed God is how we are with each other.

Morris And how would you have been with Mr Doyle if you'd sat with him in this room?

Sims I don't know, because this room, this world, has been so perverted by other people's ideas of what it should be. You and your speeches on images creating reality and why don't we make a better reality – look around! Look at this room. Look at what you've created. A place to twist people. A place to terrorise them. What did you do to Mr Doyle? Did you make him see the truth? Did you bring him to the light? Did you save him? No, actually, what you did was betray his trust, drag him from a place where he felt safe and submit him to psychological torture until he killed himself.

Morris looks around the room . . .

Morris

Sims

Morris

Sims

Morris

Sims

Morris

Sims The server is in an anchored sub off the coast of Malaysia. Latitude 4.795417, Longitude 104.567871. The server sitter's name is Jerry. He has no idea what's running on it. Don't hurt him.

Morris Thank you, Mr Sims.

Sims It doesn't matter any more.

Morris

Sims

Morris I didn't like the Hideaway. I loved it. I wanted to stay there for ever. I wanted to stay in that beautiful home with Iris. But if I had, who would I have been?

Sims Detective Morris. Is that your real name?

Morris

She begins to pack up.

Sims You're not going to return my login, are you?

Morris

Sims In-world banishment. How appropriate.

She starts to leave.

I almost did it, once. The daughter of my neighbour down the street. We would get together in person then. All of the neighbours. This was a long time ago. I couldn't stop thinking about her. She had hair the sun played in. And a laugh that came out of her like magic. I wanted to . . . get inside. I pretended to be her friend. I posed to her family as a young, harmless uncle-type. One night I got her alone in her own room. We were laughing, and I reached over and grabbed her, and she looked at me – so startled – and I . . . found it in myself to let her go. I went home, to my computer, and that's where I've stayed. You don't know what you do, Detective, putting me out into the world.

Morris The world is still the place we have to learn to be. You are free to go, Mr Sims. You are free.

She exits, leaving Sims alone.

EPILOGUE

Sims and Doyle.

Doyle Did you bring me something?

Sims Maybe . . .

Doyle Is it a birthday cake?

Sims Let's call it an Iris Day cake. It's made of ice that will never melt.

Doyle I can hear it. It's the sound of freezing and unfreezing.

Sims The cake reforms its crystal patterns.

Doyle And there's another sound. The sound of tiny dwarves who live in snowy mountains singing falsetto. Can you hear it?

Sims No. It must be only for children to hear.

Doyle Is that why you don't want me to grow up? Because I'll no longer hear the singing?

Sims Because I don't want to lose you.

Doyle It wouldn't be good for business.

Sims That's not why. You know why. Don't you?

Doyle I feel it, but . . . I do sometimes wonder if it's real.

Sims

Doyle

Sims Come here, Iris Day Girl. Did you know these trees are called poplars?

Doyle Yes.

Sims No you didn't!

Doyle Yes I did!

Overlapping 'No you didn't!' / 'Yes I did!' as they giggle.

I promise! I did!

Sims Okay, I believe you! So here's a secret: I have a garden. And guess what I just planted? A sapling. A poplar.

Doyle That's real?

Sims Real real.

Doyle Thank you.

Sims

Doyle I miss the trees.

Sims I do too.

Doyle I love you.

Sims hesitates.

Sims You cannot know how much I love you.

End.

Author's Notes

It is important to cast Iris with an actress who will appear on stage as a prepubescent girl. The child actor takes the audience *out* of the play (Bert States, *Great Reckonings in Little Rooms: On the Phenomenology of Theater,* Oakland: University of California Press, 1987), which is desirable considering the contents of her scenes. The audience is assured nothing awful will be enacted upon the child, whereas they have no such confidence with an adult posing as a child. A young actress also adds warmth, which is critical to the chemistry of the play.

There are three references that place the play in the United States of America. However, producers should feel free to make the location specific to their country. 'Franklin Middle School' should refer to a school for children around ages eleven to thirteen. 'Illinois State University' should refer to a modest, well-established public university. 'Brownstone' should refer to an historical urban dwelling, built before 1930, possibly as mass housing during the Industrial Revolution, and now typically inhabited by wealthy urbanites who can afford homes made of natural materials like stone and wood.